# ONE FLEW OVER THE CUCKOO'S NEST

by
Ken Kesey

## Student Packet

Written by
Pat Watson

Edited by
Heather M. Johnson

**Contains masters for:** 2 Prereading Activities
1 Study Guide
4 Vocabulary Activities
6 Literary Analysis Activities
4 Comprehension Activities
5 Quizzes
2 Final Tests (two levels)
**PLUS** Detailed Answer Key

---

**Note**

The Signet 1995 paperback edition of the book, published by New American Library, a division of Penguin Putnam, Inc., ©1962 by Ken Kesey, was used to prepare this guide. The page references may differ in other editions.

**Please note:** This novel deals with sensitive, mature issues. Parts may contain profanity, sexual references, and/or descriptions of violence. Please assess the appropriateness of this book for the age level and maturity of your students prior to reading and discussing it with them.

---

**ISBN 1-58130-840-X**

Copyright infringement is a violation of Federal Law.

© 2000, 2004 by Novel Units, Inc., Bulverde, Texas. All rights reserved. No part of this publication may be reproduced, translated, stored in a retrieval system, or transmitted in any way or by any means (electronic, mechanical, photocopying, recording, or otherwise) without prior written permission from Novel Units, Inc.

Photocopying of student worksheets by a classroom teacher at a non-profit school who has purchased this publication for his/her own class is permissible. Reproduction of any part of this publication for an entire school or for a school system, by for-profit institutions and tutoring centers, or for commercial sale is strictly prohibited.

Novel Units is a registered trademark of Novel Units, Inc.

Printed in the United States of America.

To order, contact your local school supply store, or—

Novel Units, Inc.
P.O. Box 97
Bulverde, TX 78163-0097

Web site: www.educyberstor.com

25 Vocab. Words (

Name _____

*One Flew Over the Cuckoo's Nest*
Activity #1 • Anticipation Guide
Use Before Reading

## Getting the "Lay of the Land"

**Directions:** Prepare for reading by answering the following questions.

1. Who is the author?

   _____

2. What does the title suggest to you about the book?

   _____
   _____
   _____
   _____

3. When was the book first copyrighted?

   _____

4. How many pages are there in the book?

   _____

5. Thumb through the book. Read three pages—one from near the beginning, one from near the middle, and one from near the end. What predictions can you make about the book?

   _____
   _____
   _____
   _____

6. What does the cover suggest to you about the book?

   _____
   _____
   _____
   _____

© Novel Units, Inc.

Name _____

*One Flew Over the Cuckoo's Nest*
Activity #2 • Anticipation Guide
Use Before Reading

**Directions:** Working with a partner, complete the following chart. Share your responses in a class discussion.

**Denotation**
_____
_____
_____

**Connotation**
_____
_____
_____

**Mental Illness**

**Synonyms**
_____
_____
_____

**Treatments**
_____
_____
_____

Name _____

*One Flew Over the Cuckoo's Nest*
Study Guide

**Directions:** Answer the following questions on a separate sheet of paper. Starred questions indicate thought or opinion questions. Use your answers in class discussions, for writing assignments, and to review for tests.

**Special Assignment:** Using the Metaphors and Similes chart on page 15 of this guide, list metaphors and similes from each section. Continue this activity on your own paper.

## Part One, pp. 9–41

1. Identify Chief Bromden, Nurse Ratched, and McMurphy and give two characteristics of each one. What is Bromden's nickname? Why?
2. *What does Bromden do when he feels threatened? What do you think this indicates about him?
3. *Identify the setting. How would you describe the atmosphere? Why?
4. Identify and explain the two classifications of patients on the ward when McMurphy arrives. Give the name of two patients in each classification. How is McMurphy classified?
5. *What metaphors does the narrator use to describe the hospital and the ward? What does this suggest to you?
6. What is Nurse Ratched's objective for each of the patients? What methods does she use to achieve this?
7. Who is Mr. Taber? Why does Nurse Ratched consider him to be a success story?
8. *Prediction: How will McMurphy keep the hospital from running smoothly?

## pp. 42–69

1. Describe how Nurse Ratched manipulates the patients during the first Group Meeting McMurphy attends. What is Bromden tempted to do? Why doesn't he do so?
2. What does Ratched reveal about McMurphy? How does McMurphy react to her?
3. Why has McMurphy been sent to the mental hospital?
4. *Describe Dr. Spivey and explain whether or not you think he is competent.
5. *To what does McMurphy compare the Group Meeting? Explain what you think this means.
6. To what does Harding compare the patients? Why does he do so?
7. *How do the men react after the Group Meeting? Why are they all afraid to oppose Nurse Ratched? How do you think this affects McMurphy?
8. What does McMurphy wager he can do in one week? How much does each man bet?
9. Why does the author, Ken Kesey, capitalize phrases like "Group Meeting"?
10. *Prediction: Will McMurphy win the wager? How?

Name _____

*One Flew Over the Cuckoo's Nest*
Study Guide
page 2

## pp. 70–101

1. Identify three indications that Chief Bromden suffers from a serious mental illness.
2. *What does Bromden think is inside Blastic when the men cut him open? What do you think this symbolizes?
3. How does McMurphy react to the patients? How does his arrival affect the patients and staff? How does he initially affect Bromden?
4. What does Harding reveal to McMurphy about life on the ward?
5. *Describe McMurphy's shorts and explain what you think they symbolize.
6. What does McMurphy do that causes Ratched to lose her composure?
7. *Identify three changes McMurphy attempts to achieve on the ward. What is he able to achieve? What do you think this reveals about him?
8. What do McMurphy and Dr. Spivey discover they have in common? How does this affect life on the ward?

## pp. 102–128

1. *Following Rawler's suicide, what do you think Bromden means by saying "all the guy had to do was wait" (p. 115)?
2. How does Bromden correlate his "fog" with his experiences in WWII? Why does he try not to get too deeply immersed in his mental fog?
3. Relating to the fog, what does Bromden think McMurphy is trying to do to the men? Why does this upset him?
4. Why does McMurphy become angry and lose control during the first discussion about watching the World Series? How does he retaliate against the patients?
5. How does McMurphy suggest the men escape? What does he think will be effective in this plan?
6. *When did Billy Bibbit first start stuttering? How has this affected his life? What do you think this signifies?
7. *What happens in the second vote concerning the World Series? What do you think this reveals about McMurphy, Bromden, and Ratched?
8. *What is the final outcome of the conflict over the World Series? Explain whether or not you think McMurphy "wins."
9. ***Prediction:** Will McMurphy succeed in uniting the patients against Nurse Ratched?

Name _____

*One Flew Over the Cuckoo's Nest*
Study Guide
page 3

## Part Two, pp. 129–151

1. How does Nurse Ratched retaliate against McMurphy for staging the silent protest? How do the patients continue their protest?
2. How does Bromden learn what goes on in the staff meetings? Why is he allowed to be there?
3. *What does Bromden believe he must clean up after the staff meetings? What do you think this symbolizes?
4. What does the staff doctor tell the staff about McMurphy? What do the residents conclude about him? To what three historic figures does one of the residents compare him?
5. *What does Nurse Ratched intend to do with McMurphy? Why? Explain why you do or do not think her plan will succeed.
6. Briefly explain McMurphy's effect on Bromden.
7. What does McMurphy learn that causes him to become submissive to Nurse Ratched? How does he act differently? What effect does this have on the other patients?

## pp. 152–173

1. What happens to Sefelt? Why does this happen? How does Ratched use this to warn the other patients?
2. Describe Vera Harding. How does Harding react when she comes to visit?
3. *How does Vera Harding treat her husband? What do you think this indicates about their relationship?
4. *What does McMurphy see in his bad dreams? What do you think these dreams symbolize?
5. What does Harding tell McMurphy about Electro-Shock Therapy? about a lobotomy?
6. Identify the metaphor Harding uses to describe EST. What does he mean by this?
7. How does McMurphy classify Nurse Ratched to the other patients?
8. How does McMurphy explain his rationale for changing his tactics with Ratched? How do the men react?
9. *What causes McMurphy to resume hostilities with Ratched? What does he do in retaliation? Why do you think he does this?
10. ***Prediction:** Who will win in the conflict between McMurphy and Ratched? How?

*One Flew Over the Cuckoo's Nest*
Study Guide
page 4

### Part Three, pp. 174–190

1. *How do McMurphy and Ratched treat each other after he shatters the window? What do you think this reveals about both of them?

2. What is Ratched's response to McMurphy's first request for an Accompanied Pass? What does McMurphy then do?

3. *Identify two ways McMurphy harasses Ratched. Which one of these do you think most irritates her?

4. Who becomes McMurphy's ally in trying to improve the lives of the patients? How does he help?

5. What does McMurphy plan to do when his second request for an Accompanied Pass is granted? Who will be the chaperones? What does Ratched do to counteract McMurphy's plans?

6. *Explain what you think Bromden means by his statement, "…it wasn't me that started acting deaf; it was people that first started acting like I was too dumb to hear or see or say anything at all" (p. 178). Have you ever experienced a similar feeling? If so, what was the occasion, and how did you react?

7. Identify two things from Bromden's past that have caused him to feel incompetent and unnoticed.

8. What does Bromden tell McMurphy about his father and mother? What caused his father's death?

9. *Explain what you think Bromden means when he refers to the Combine.

10. *What happens that causes Bromden to speak to McMurphy? What does Bromden say? Why do you think this is significant?

11. What does McMurphy offer Bromden if he can lift the control panel?

12. ***Prediction:** Will McMurphy succeed in taking the men fishing?

### pp. 191–218

1. *Who does McMurphy sign up as the ninth man for the fishing trip? How do you think this makes both of them feel?

2. Why doesn't George Sorensen want to go on the fishing trip? How does McMurphy manipulate him into going?

3. What complication arises before the men can leave? How is it resolved?

4. *How do the men at the service station initially treat the patients? How does McMurphy handle the situation? Explain why you do or do not think public reaction to mental illness has changed.

Name _____

*One Flew Over the Cuckoo's Nest*
Study Guide
page 5

5. *Why does the boat captain refuse to take the men out in the boat? How does McMurphy solve the problem? Explain whether you think his actions are right or wrong.

6. *What changes occur in the men during the fishing trip? Why do you think they change?

7. *How does Dr. Spivey avert a problem with the police after the men return to the dock? What do you think this reveals about him?

8. *What has Bromden noticed about McMurphy throughout the day of the fishing trip? What do you think this indicates about McMurphy?

9. What plan does McMurphy intend to help Billy Bibbit arrange?

## Part Four, pp. 219–241

1. Briefly explain Nurse Ratched's next maneuver and how it affects the men.

2. *How does McMurphy react to the men's subtle accusations? What do you think this reveals about him?

3. During a Group Meeting when McMurphy is absent, what does Ratched tell the men about him? What sways Bibbit and Bromden to question his motives?

4. *Explain what you think Bromden means by the metaphor, "…McMurphy was a giant" (p. 224).

5. How far is Bromden able to move the control panel? What does McMurphy then do that causes Bromden to feel differently about him?

6. What is Nurse Ratched's pretense for ordering special showers for the men who went on the fishing trip?

7. What causes McMurphy to attack Washington? Who joins him in the conflict? What is the immediate result?

8. Contrast the nurse on the Disturbed Ward with Nurse Ratched. What does she tell McMurphy and Bromden about Ratched?

9. *How can McMurphy avoid EST? Why do you think he refuses?

10. *Explain your interpretation of the rhyme Bromden remembers from his childhood as he is about to receive EST (p. 239).

## pp. 242–259

1. *How does Bromden's reaction to EST differ from previous times? Why do you think this is so? What is significant about this treatment?

2. What does McMurphy tell Bromden about his treatments? What physical signs does Bromden observe in McMurphy before each EST?

Name _____

*One Flew Over the Cuckoo's Nest*
Study Guide
page 6

3. Why does Ratched have McMurphy returned to the ward? How does he act when he returns?

4. What do the other men want McMurphy to do? How do they plan to achieve this?

5. Briefly describe the Saturday night party on the ward.

6. *What is revealed about Billy Bibbit's mother? Why do you think this information is significant?

7. *What does Fredrickson sprinkle over Sefelt and Sandra? What do you think this symbolizes?

8. *Prediction: What will happen to McMurphy? to Nurse Ratched? to the other patients?

## pp. 260–272

1. In the aftermath of the party, what does Nurse Ratched threaten to do concerning Billy Bibbit's actions?

2. What happens to Billy? Who does Nurse Ratched blame? Explain the irony of her accusations.

3. How does the conflict between McMurphy and Ratched end?

4. Describe Nurse Ratched's physical and mental condition when she returns to the ward. What happens to most of her patients?

5. *What is Nurse Ratched's "final play"? What effect does she expect this to have on the other patients? How does Bromden foil her plan? Why do you think he does this?

6. Explain what happens to Bromden in the denouement.

7. In retrospect, what does Bromden believe about the events in the denouement?

Name _____

*One Flew Over the Cuckoo's Nest*
Activity #3 • Vocabulary
Part One, pp. 9–128

| cagey (10) | psychopath (18) | therapeutic (19) | bent (24) |
| philosophy (29) | neurology (31) | insubordination (44) | protocol (47) |
| prototype (48) | sadistic (56) | veritable (58) | ethereally (58) |
| benevolence (58) | matriarchy (59) | astute (61) | juggernaut (66) |
| impregnable (67) | stoicism (73) | uncanny (75) | geriatrics (89) |
| infernal (95) | maudlin (97) | apathy (107) | interceptors (116) |

**Directions:** Choose 20 vocabulary words from the list above and complete the chart.

| Word | Part of Speech | Synonym | Antonym |
|---|---|---|---|
| | | | |
| | | | |
| | | | |
| | | | |
| | | | |
| | | | |
| | | | |
| | | | |
| | | | |
| | | | |
| | | | |
| | | | |
| | | | |
| | | | |
| | | | |
| | | | |
| | | | |
| | | | |
| | | | |
| | | | |

Name _____

*One Flew Over the Cuckoo's Nest*
Activity #4 • Vocabulary
Part Two, pp. 129–173

✓ Marked words

| *arch type (134) | schizophrenic (135) | latent (135) | Oedipal (135) |
|---|---|---|---|
| blowhard (136) | silage (141) | — impound (146) | hydrocephalus (149) |
| lymph (149) | kneading (153) | schematic (157) | — curtail (158) |
| nemesis (158) | — punitive (163) | lobotomy (163) | aplomb (163) |
| vogue (164) | — lucid (165) | spoor (169) | — circumvent (171) |

*spelling in novel

**Directions:** Circle the word that does not belong in each of the following lists. On a separate piece of paper, briefly explain why the circled word does not belong.

| | | | | |
|---|---|---|---|---|
| 1. **arch type** | original | paragon | cupola | ideal |
| 2. **schizophrenic** | deviation | conformity | psychotic | disassociation |
| 3. **latent** | evident | inactive | dormant | concealed |
| 4. **Oedipal** | attachment | literary | psychoneurosis | obsession |
| 5. **blowhard** | boaster | self-denigrating | exhibitionist | braggart |
| 6. **silage** | fodder | silence | ensilage | feed |
| ✓ 7. **impound** | liberate | seize | confine | confiscate |
| 8. **hydrocephalus** | fluid | cerebrospinal | cranium | hydrophobia |
| 9. **lymph** | liquid | body | corpuscle | colorless |
| 10. **kneading** | shaping | manipulate | squeeze | essential |
| 11. **schematic** | diagram | automatic | pattern | plan |
| ✓ 12. **curtail** | diminish | expand | reduce | abate |
| 13. **nemesis** | punishment | vengeance | mercy | retaliation |
| ✓ 14. **punitive** | punishment | castigation | abusive | inoffensive |
| 15. **lobotomy** | laboratory | surgery | invasive | brain |
| 16. **aplomb** | confidence | poise | defamation | intrepidity |
| ✓ 17. **vogue** | popularity | acceptance | prevalence | noncompliance |
| ✓ 18. **lucid** | imprudent | sane | rational | sagacious |
| 19. **spoor** | trail | track | fungi | animal |
| ✓ 20. **circumvent** | avoid | enclose | sidestep | elude |

Name _____

*One Flew Over the Cuckoo's Nest*
Activity #5 • Vocabulary
Part Three, pp. 174–218

| hovel (180) | fraternize (180) | squalor (180) | indigents (189) |
| keelhaul (192) | wistful (192) | turret (204) | cormorants (210) |

**Directions:** Complete the following analogies, using the vocabulary words from the list above.

1. PALATIAL is to MANSION as CRUDE is to _____.

2. ACCOLADE is to TRIBUTE as PUNISHMENT is to _____.

3. MIX is to COMBINE as CONSORT is to _____.

4. TRANSPARENT is to OPAQUE as CLEANLINESS is to _____.

5. REPTILES are to SNAKES as BIRDS are to _____.

6. MEDICINE is to PHARMACY as GUNS are to _____.

7. AFFLUENT is to TYCOONS as DESTITUTE is to _____.

8. DEPRESSED is to CAREFREE as BLISSFUL is to _____.

Name _____

**One Flew Over the Cuckoo's Nest**
Activity #6 • Vocabulary
Part Four, pp. 219–272

| philanthropy (222) | capitalistic (223) | chicanery (223) | effrontery (223) |
| provocative (248) | chastising (258) | shellacked (261) | atrocities (262) |
| discretion (264) | contemptuous (265) | skittered (268) | syndicate (272) |

**Directions:** Match each vocabulary word with the word or phrase closest in meaning.

____ 1. philanthropy           a. brutalities

____ 2. capitalistic           b. stimulating

____ 3. chicanery              c. good judgment

____ 4. effrontery             d. controlling organization

____ 5. provocative            e. benevolence

____ 6. chastising             f. moved lightly

____ 7. shellacked             g. impudence

____ 8. atrocities             h. varnished

____ 9. discretion             i. entrepreneurial

____ 10. contemptuous          j. rebuking

____ 11. skittered             k. disdainful

____ 12. syndicate             l. deception

Name _____

*One Flew Over the Cuckoo's Nest*
Activity #7 • Literary Analysis
Use During and After Reading

# Metaphors and Similes

A **metaphor** is a comparison between two unlike objects. For example, "he was a human tree." A **simile** is a comparison between two unlike objects that uses the words *like* or *as*. For example, "the color of her eyes was like the cloudless sky."

**Directions:** Complete the chart below by listing metaphors and similes from the novel, as well as the page numbers on which they are found. Identify metaphors with an "M" and similes with an "S." Translate the comparisons in your own words, and then list the objects being compared.

| Metaphors/Similes | Ideas/Objects Being Compared |
|---|---|
| 1. <br><br>Translation: | |
| 2. <br><br>Translation: | |
| 3. <br><br>Translation: | |

Name _____

*One Flew Over the Cuckoo's Nest*
Activity #8 • Character Analysis
Use During and After Reading

# Character Web

**Directions:** Write "McMurphy" in the center box and complete the chart. Cite evidence from the story as you fill in the information.

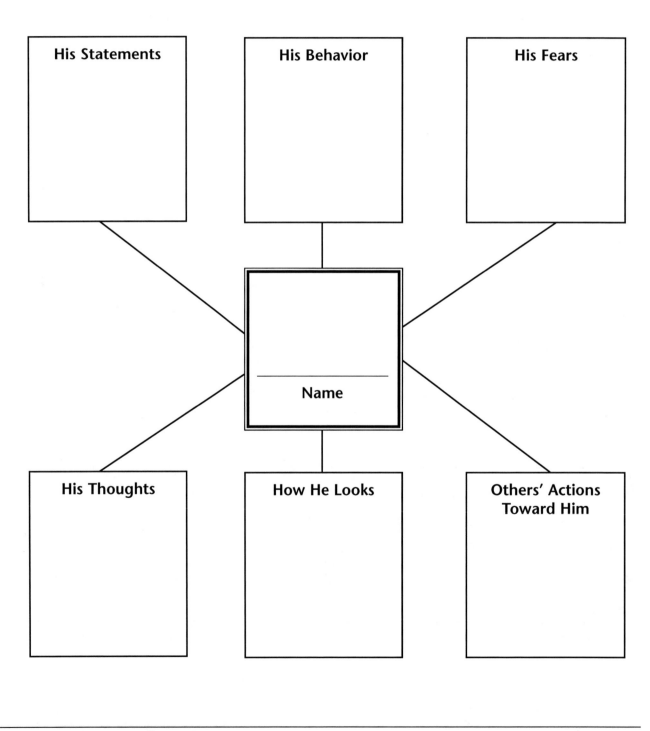

Name _____

*One Flew Over the Cuckoo's Nest*
Activity #9 • Character Analysis
Use During and After Reading

## Character Analysis Blocks

**Directions:** Analyze Nurse Ratched by completing the graphic below.

| | Who is the character? | |
|---|---|---|
| | **What does the character do?** | **Why does s/he do it?** |
| What, if anything, is significant about the character's name? | What is the nature of this character's actions? (reactive, active, important, consequential, secondary) | What is the significance of the book's time and place to the character? |
| What is unusual or important about the character? | How does the character change in the story? | Does the character remind you of another character from another book? Who? | Do you know anyone similar to this character? |

© Novel Units, Inc.

Name _____

**One Flew Over the Cuckoo's Nest**
ACTIVITY #10 • Character Analysis
Use During and After Reading

## Feelings

**Directions:** Complete the following chart to characterize Chief Bromden.

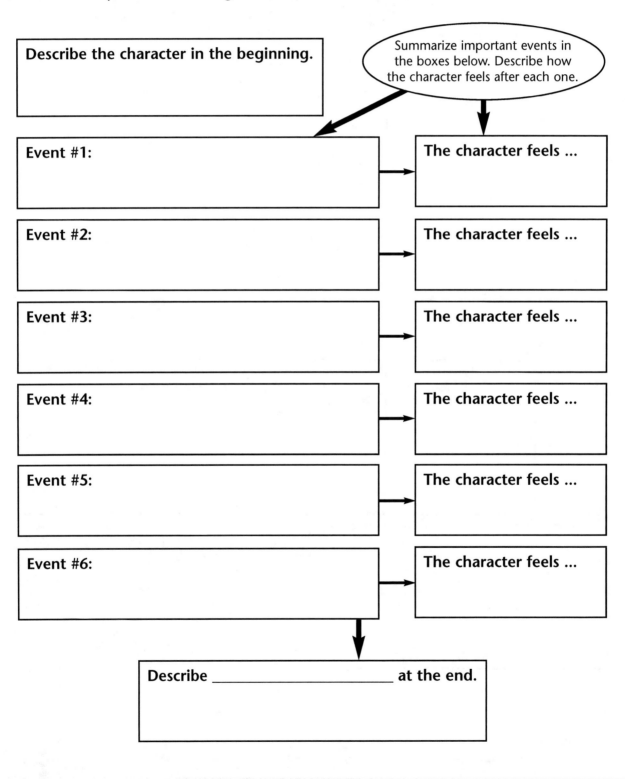

Name _____

*One Flew Over the Cuckoo's Nest*
Activity #11 • Character Analysis
Use During and After Reading

## Character Analysis

**Directions:** Working in small groups, discuss the attributes of the characters listed below. In each character's box, write several words or phrases that describe him or her.

Name _____

*One Flew Over the Cuckoo's Nest*
Activity #12 • Plot Analysis
Use During and After Reading

# Story Map

**Directions:** Fill in each box below with information about the novel.

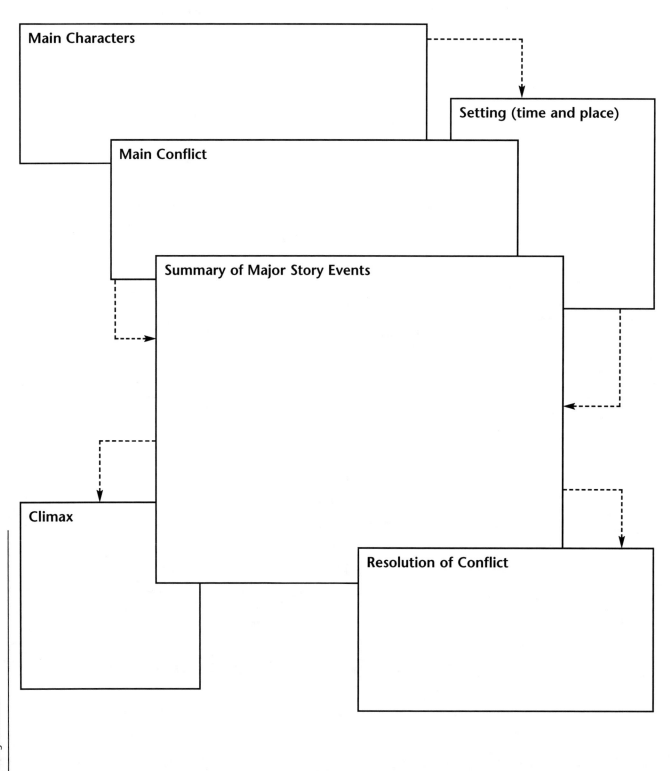

**One Flew Over the Cuckoo's Nest**
Activity #13 • Comprehension
Use After Reading

Name _____

## Fishbone Map

**Directions:** List "McMurphy's Death" as the result. Consider the causes. List cause 1, 2, 3, 4 (as appropriate). Add details to support the causes you list.

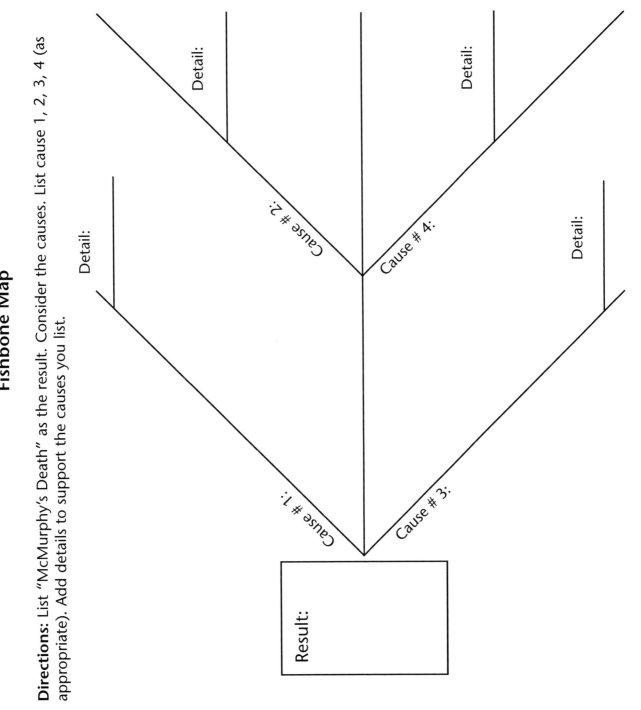

Name _____

**One Flew Over the Cuckoo's Nest**
Activity #14 • Comprehension
Use After Reading

## Inference Flow Chart

**Directions:** Fill in the boxes of the flow chart with the events portrayed in the story. In the ovals beneath, state what emotions and feelings are inferred.

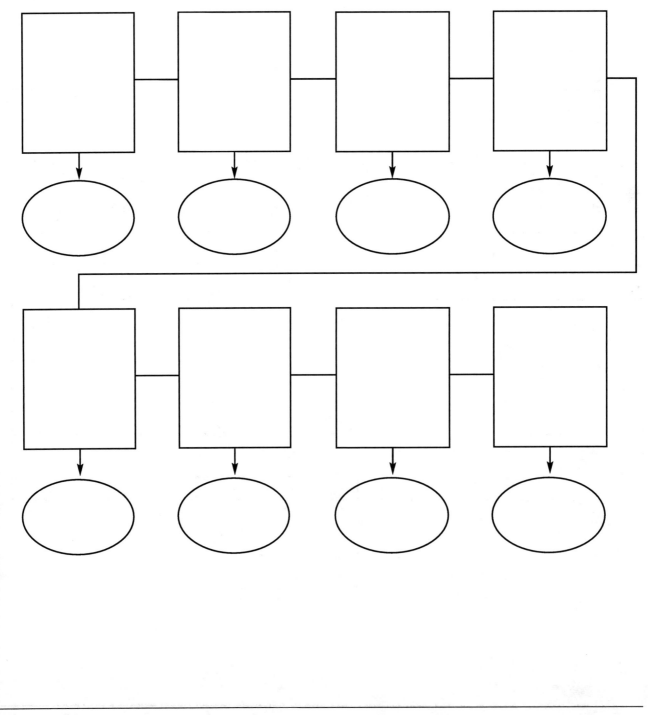

Name _____

*One Flew Over the Cuckoo's Nest*
Activity #15 • Comprehension
Use After Reading

## Making Decisions

**Directions:** Choose three to five possible solutions to the problem below.

(a) State each solution in a short sentence.

(b) Design three to five "criteria" (questions you can ask to measure how good a particular choice may be).

(c) Rate the criteria for each solution: 1 = yes; 2 = maybe; 3 = no.

**Problem:** Problems at the state mental hospital need to be corrected.

| Solutions ↓ | Criteria | | | | |
|---|---|---|---|---|---|
| 1. | | | | | |
| 2. | | | | | |
| 3. | | | | | |
| 4. | | | | | |
| 5. | | | | | |

Name _____

*One Flew Over the Cuckoo's Nest*
Activity #16 • Comprehension
Use After Reading

## Protagonists and Antagonists

The main character in a story is called the **protagonist**. Sometimes we call the protagonist the hero or heroine (the "good" person). The character who opposes the hero in a story is called the **antagonist**. Sometimes we call the antagonist the villain (the "bad" person).

**Directions:** Think about stories you have read. Who were some of the protagonists (heroes/heroines) in these stories? Who were the antagonists (villains)? List some of the protagonists and antagonists and the stories in which they appeared.

| Protagonists | Antagonists | Story |
|---|---|---|
|  |  |  |
|  |  |  |
|  |  |  |
|  |  |  |

Complete the charts below by listing some common characteristics of protagonists and antagonists. For example, a protagonist is often brave. An antagonist may be cunning or cruel. Sometimes the antagonist is not just a person but a belief or custom.

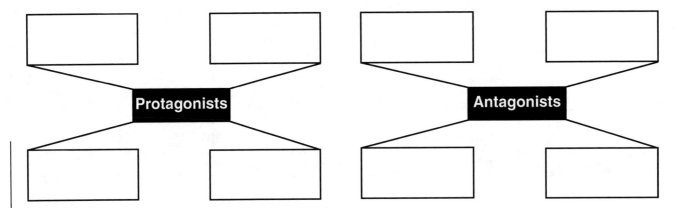

As you read *One Flew Over the Cuckoo's Nest*, decide who is the protagonist and who or what is the antagonist. Notice their characteristics and compare/contrast them to the characters you listed in the chart above.

Name _____

**One Flew Over the Cuckoo's Nest**
Quiz #1
Part One, pp. 9–69

## Matching

____ 1. chooses mental hospital over prison work farm     a. Billy Bibbit

____ 2. narrator of the novel     b. Dr. Spivey

____ 3. manipulates the patients through fear     c. Dale Harding

____ 4. is subservient due to fear of being fired     d. Chief Bromden

____ 5. president of the Patient's Council     e. R.P. McMurphy

____ 6. has a severe stuttering problem     f. Nurse Ratched

## True/False

____ 7. Chief Bromden believes Nurse Ratched to be an Angel of Mercy.

____ 8. Bromden retreats into a mental fog to escape reality.

____ 9. When McMurphy first arrives at the hospital, he is incoherent.

____ 10. McMurphy is committed to the mental hospital for possible psychopathy.

____ 11. Nurse Ratched quickly classifies McMurphy as a manipulator.

____ 12. Nurse Ratched chooses the black boys as her aides because of their compassion.

____ 13. Dr. Spivey's primary function in the Group Meetings is to order specific treatment for the patients.

____ 14. Harding compares the patients in the hospital to rabbits.

____ 15. McMurphy's first wager with the other patients is that he can "get her [Nurse Ratched's] goat" in one week.

Name _____

**One Flew Over the Cuckoo's Nest**
Quiz #2
Part One, pp. 70–128

**Fill in the Blanks**

1. Nurse Pilbow is afraid of McMurphy because Nurse Ratched tells her _____.

2. Bromden classifies the controlling forces of society as a _____.

3. Patients on the ward are astounded when they awaken to hear McMurphy _____.

4. McMurphy's undershorts are covered with _____.

5. The power struggle between Nurse Ratched and McMurphy begins when he asks permission to _____.

6. One staff member, _____, supports McMurphy in his request for change.

7. In the first vote for the right to watch the World Series, most of the patients refuse to vote because _____.

8. McMurphy suggests escaping by _____.

9. Billy Bibbit first stuttered when he tried to say the word _____.

10. After Nurse Ratched thwarts the patients' second vote to watch the World Series, they retaliate by_____.

Name _____

*One Flew Over the Cuckoo's Nest*
Quiz #3
Part Two, pp. 129–173

## True/False

___ 1. Chief Bromden is allowed in the staff room during meetings because everyone thinks he is deaf.

___ 2. Nurse Ratched punishes McMurphy for rebelling over the vote to watch the World Series by assigning him to kitchen duty.

___ 3. Cheswick is taken to the Disturbed Ward after demanding that something be done about cigarette rationing.

___ 4. The other patients angrily confront McMurphy when he begins to conform to Nurse Ratched's orders.

___ 5. Vera Harding's visit to her husband ends in reconciliation.

___ 6. Most of the admitted patients remain because they don't have the courage to leave.

## Short Answer

7. To what does Bromden compare the talk about patients that occurs in the staff room?

8. What is Nurse Ratched's rationale for not sending McMurphy to the Disturbed Ward?

9. What is the primary indication that Bromden is emerging from his mental illness?

10. What causes McMurphy to change his behavior toward Nurse Ratched?

11. What two types of treatment does Harding describe for McMurphy?

12. What is the first thing Nurse Ratched does to provoke McMurphy's anger, and what does he do in retaliation?

Name _____

**One Flew Over the Cuckoo's Nest**
Quiz #4
Part Three, pp. 174–218

## Fill in the Blanks

1. McMurphy organizes a _____ team for the patients.

2. Bromden first begins to talk to McMurphy after _____
   _____.

3. Bromden tells McMurphy that his father fought the "Combine" until _____
   _____.

4. In exchange for the $10.00 fee for the fishing trip, McMurphy asks Bromden to
   _____.

5. _____ and _____ are chaperones for the patients on their fishing trip.

## Short Answer

6. Why does McMurphy break the window in the Nurses' Station for the second time?

7. How does Nurse Ratched counteract McMurphy's planned fishing trip for the patients?

8. What has caused Bromden to act deaf?

9. How does McMurphy convince Sorensen to join the group for the fishing trip?

10. Why are policemen waiting when the group returns from fishing? How do the men avoid trouble?

Name _____

**One Flew Over the Cuckoo's Nest**
Quiz #5
Part Four, pp. 219–272

**True/False**

____ 1. After the fishing trip, Nurse Ratched begins to spread rumors about McMurphy's motives.

____ 2. Bromden feels betrayed by McMurphy because of his wager with the other patients over Bromden's ability to lift the control panel.

____ 3. McMurphy reaches the breaking point in his conflict with Nurse Ratched over the way her aides treat Bromden.

____ 4. Nurse Ratched orders shock therapy for McMurphy after he strikes her.

____ 5. Bromden knows he is emerging from insanity when he conquers his desire to slip off into the fog after an EST treatment.

____ 6. McMurphy arranges for a Saturday night visit from Candy because of Billy Bibbit.

____ 7. Harding's ingenuity prevents the supervisor from learning about the party.

____ 8. McMurphy unsuccessfully attempts to escape before the aides come on duty the morning after the party.

____ 9. Nurse Ratched humiliates Billy by threatening to tell Dr. Spivey about his behavior with Candy.

____ 10. McMurphy attacks Nurse Ratched after Billy commits suicide.

**Short Answer:** Briefly explain what happens to each of the following in the resolution of the novel.

11. McMurphy:

12. Nurse Ratched:

13. Chief Bromden:

14. Harding:

15. Sorensen:

Name _____

*One Flew Over the Cuckoo's Nest*
Final Test, Level One

**A. Identification:** Match each character with the correct identification. (1 point each)

____ 1. loud, strong, bold protagonist
____ 2. large, half-Indian narrator
____ 3. stern, unfeeling, manipulative antagonist
____ 4. begins to rally for the patients
____ 5. college graduate; dominated by wife
____ 6. shy, repressed patient who stutters
____ 7. prostitute; comes to the party on the ward
____ 8. obsessed with cleanliness
____ 9. night aide who helps plan the party
____ 10. taunts her husband with subtle criticisms

a. Nurse Ratched
b. Dale Harding
c. George Sorensen
d. Randle Patrick McMurphy
e. Dr. Spivey
f. Candy
g. Mr. Turkle
h. Vera Harding
i. Chief Bromden
j. Billy Bibbit

**B. Multiple Choice:** Choose the BEST answer. (2 points each)

____ 11. Chief Bromden is nicknamed "Chief Broom" because
  (a) he is tall and thin
  (b) he pretends to be a broom
  (c) he sweeps the ward
  (d) he was a janitor before becoming mentally ill

____ 12. Most of the novel is narrated
  (a) from a child's viewpoint
  (b) as a flashback
  (c) as a letter to the hospital supervisor
  (d) from McMurphy's point of view

____ 13. McMurphy indicates that he is no ordinary admission by
  (a) his lack of fear
  (b) his apparel
  (c) the amount of money he has
  (d) his arrival by ambulance

____ 14. The Combine symbolizes
  (a) Electro Shock Therapy
  (b) a lobotomy
  (c) the controlling factions of society
  (d) McMurphy's gambling operation

Name _____

*One Flew Over the Cuckoo's Nest*
Final Test, Level One
page 2

____ 15. One method by which Nurse Ratched controls the patients on her ward is
(a) threatening to dismiss them too early
(b) allowing her aides to beat them
(c) making them stand against the wall for hours
(d) publicly humiliating them

____ 16. Nurse Ratched classifies McMurphy as
(a) an interrogator
(b) a manipulator
(c) dogmatic
(d) liberated

____ 17. A predominant sign of the oppressive atmosphere on the ward is
(a) no one wants to eat
(b) patients are in a stupor
(c) patients have no communication with each other
(d) no one laughs

____ 18. McMurphy compares the Group Meetings to
(a) a chicken's pecking party
(b) a gossip session
(c) solitary confinement
(d) an FBI interrogation

____ 19. McMurphy recognizes Nurse Ratched's ability to
(a) help the patients confront their fears
(b) cause a patient to have a seizure
(c) emasculate the patients emotionally
(d) cause the patients to become addicted to prescription drugs

____ 20. Harding's description of the EST table is an example of
(a) personification
(b) hallucination
(c) flashback
(d) symbolism

____ 21. Bromden's insanity is depicted by his
(a) uncontrollable rage
(b) fog-covered solitude
(c) inability to hear
(d) stuttering

Name _____

One Flew Over the Cuckoo's Nest
Final Test, Level One
page 3

____ 22. The Acute patients first realize McMurphy is different when
(a) they awaken to hear him singing
(b) he challenges Nurse Ratched over her clothing
(c) he arranges a fishing trip for them
(d) he gets Bromden to speak

____ 23. An initial indication that the power struggle between McMurphy and Nurse Ratched has started is when
(a) she reveals his background to the other patients
(b) he breaks the window at the Nurses' Station
(c) she rejects his request to allow the card players to use another room
(d) he refuses to attend the Group Meeting

____ 24. McMurphy finds an ally against Nurse Ratched when Dr. Spivey
(a) tells her McMurphy is not mentally ill
(b) supports his suggestions for change
(c) asks her to resign
(d) cancels the Group Meetings

____ 25. Most of the Acute patients refuse to vote to watch the World Series because
(a) they would rather watch the news
(b) they don't want their routine interrupted
(c) McMurphy seems too controlling
(d) they are afraid Nurse Ratched will make things worse for them

____ 26. Evidence of Billy Bibbit's mental illness includes all BUT which of the following?
(a) stuttering
(b) hallucinating
(c) attempting suicide
(d) inflicting pain on himself

____ 27. Bromden's first obvious effort to associate with the other patients occurs when he
(a) speaks to McMurphy
(b) reveals secrets he's heard from staff members
(c) votes to watch the World Series
(d) offers to help Harding

____ 28. When the staff members suggest sending McMurphy to the Disturbed Ward, Nurse Ratched rejects the idea because
(a) she doesn't want the other patients to view him as a martyr
(b) they have misdiagnosed him as schizophrenic
(c) she secretly likes him
(d) she thinks it will make him more deranged

Name _____

*One Flew Over the Cuckoo's Nest*
Final Test, Level One
page 4

____ 29. One of the first positive signs that Bromden is beginning to regain his sanity is his
   (a) refusal to sweep
   (b) refusal to take his medicine
   (c) ability to hear again
   (d) ability to see clearly

____ 30. McMurphy becomes submissive to Nurse Ratched's domination
   (a) when she threatens him with EST
   (b) after he learns she controls his release date
   (c) because the other patients are too apathetic
   (d) when he decides to return to the work farm

____ 31. Harding compares a lobotomy to
   (a) crucifixion
   (b) castration
   (c) annihilation
   (d) death

____ 32. Most of the patients who could leave the hospital voluntarily do not do so because
   (a) they do not have the courage
   (b) they do not have enough money
   (c) family members refuse to help them
   (d) they have become drug dependent

____ 33. A major turning point in the relationship between McMurphy and Nurse Ratched occurs
   (a) after his return from EST
   (b) when she will not allow him to gamble with the men
   (c) before Cheswick drowns
   (d) when she takes away the men's privilege to use the tub room for card games

____ 34. Nurse Ratched attempts to defeat McMurphy's plans for the fishing trip by
   (a) convincing Dr. Spivey that it is dangerous
   (b) posting clippings about tragic boat accidents
   (c) refusing to give her permission
   (d) refusing to release the patients' money

____ 35. McMurphy promises to make Bromden "big" again and to pay his $10.00 fee for the fishing trip if he will
   (a) promise to lift the control panel
   (b) agree to go on the fishing trip
   (c) prove to the aides that he can hear and talk
   (d) promise not to let the others know he can hear

Name _____

*One Flew Over the Cuckoo's Nest*
Final Test, Level One
page 5

____ 36. From the patients' perspective, the fishing trip is best described as
(a) unsuccessful
(b) partially successful
(c) completely successful
(d) too threatening

____ 37. Nurse Ratched undermines McMurphy's influence by
(a) reminding the men of her ability to make life harder for them
(b) posting a statement of their financial dealings since McMurphy's arrival
(c) telling the men that he is a thief
(d) reminding them that he is a psychopath

____ 38. McMurphy attacks Washington
(a) in retaliation for all the things Washington has done to him
(b) because he torments everyone
(c) after Billy Bibbit's suicide
(d) because he humiliates Sorensen

____ 39. McMurphy can avoid EST treatments if
(a) Bromden will say he instigated the attack
(b) Dr. Spivey will defend him
(c) he will admit he was wrong
(d) he will beg for Ratched's forgiveness

____ 40. After McMurphy returns to the ward, the other patients want him to
(a) escape
(b) admit his error to Nurse Ratched
(c) cancel Candy's visit
(d) return their money

____ 41. Which of the following does NOT occur during the Saturday night party?
(a) Mr. Turkle assists the patients.
(b) McMurphy unsuccessfully tries to escape.
(c) Billy sleeps with Candy.
(d) The patients get drunk.

____ 42. McMurphy attacks Nurse Ratched because
(a) she orders him to undergo a lobotomy
(b) she refuses his sexual advances
(c) he becomes irrational after EST
(d) he blames her for Billy Bibbit's suicide

Name _____

*One Flew Over the Cuckoo's Nest*
Final Test, Level One
page 6

____ 43. Which of the following does NOT occur in the resolution of the novel?
(a) Ratched regains total control of the ward.
(b) Ratched loses most of her patients.
(c) Bromden escapes.
(d) Bromden kills McMurphy.

____ 44. Her face "became soft and runny like melting chocolate" is an example of
(a) metaphor
(b) personification
(c) simile
(d) allusion

____ 45. "Billy Bibbit is a rabbit" is an example of
(a) simile
(b) allegory
(c) personification
(d) metaphor

**C. Essay:** Choose one of the following and respond in a well-developed essay of at least three paragraphs. (10 points)

(a) Explain how and why Bromden changes during the novel.

(b) Trace the development of either the theme "sacrifice" or "courage" in the novel.

(c) Explain the conflict between McMurphy and Nurse Ratched.

**D. Creative Response:** Choose one of the following. (10 points)

(a) Write a letter from Bromden to Candy after McMurphy's death.

(b) Write a poem about one of the emotions Nurse Ratched evokes in her patients.

(c) Write a eulogy for McMurphy.

Name _____

**One Flew Over the Cuckoo's Nest**
Final Test, Level Two

**A. Identification:** Write two to four words that characterize each of the following. (1 point each)

1. Randle Patrick McMurphy:

2. Chief Bromden:

3. Nurse Ratched:

4. Dale Harding:

5. Billy Bibbit:

6. Dr. Spivey:

7. Vera Harding:

8. George Sorensen:

9. Geever, Washington, and Williams:

10. Nurse Pilbow:

**B. Multiple Choice:** Choose the BEST answer. (1 point each)

____ 11. Which of the following is NOT true of Chief Bromden?
(a) His nickname is "Chief Broom."
(b) He is a WWII veteran.
(c) He is a deaf mute.
(d) He narrates the story in retrospect.

____ 12. Indications that McMurphy is no ordinary admission to the hospital include all BUT which of the following?
(a) He is not afraid.
(b) He brashly announces his arrival to the other patients.
(c) He shakes hands with everyone but Sorensen.
(d) He immediately explains why he has been committed.

____ 13. Nurse Ratched classifies McMurphy as a manipulator because she believes he desires all BUT which of the following?
(a) avoidance of prison
(b) a comfortable, easy life
(c) respect and power
(d) monetary gain

Name _____

*One Flew Over the Cuckoo's Nest*
Final Test, Level Two
page 2

____ 14. Signs of Nurse Ratched's control include all BUT which of the following?
(a) No one laughs.
(b) Patients spy on each other.
(c) Patients are addicted to prescription drugs.
(d) No one defends himself in Group Meetings.

____ 15. Evidence of Bromden's insanity include all BUT which of the following?
(a) He believes Big Nurse can set the clock at any speed she wishes.
(b) He believes himself to be an arthropod.
(c) He believes machinery is located in the walls.
(d) He believes the dorm floor slides.

____ 16. McMurphy does all BUT which of the following in his efforts to improve the patients' lives?
(a) asks Nurse Ratched to reduce the amount of medication
(b) tries to get the volume of the music turned down
(c) asks to be allowed to move the card game to another room
(d) begins plans for a carnival

____ 17. The "war of wills" between McMurphy and Ratched escalates intensely after
(a) he begins to gamble with the men
(b) she refuses to allow him to speak in the Group Meeting
(c) she reveals information about his past
(d) the second vote to watch the World Series

____ 18. The staff's conclusion during a meeting concerning whether or not McMurphy is an ordinary man is an example of
(a) sarcasm
(b) allusion
(c) irony
(d) hyperbole

____ 19. McMurphy resumes hostilities with Nurse Ratched after
(a) he realizes he has no chance of being released
(b) she takes away the men's privilege of using the tub room for card games
(c) the other patients beg him to do so
(d) she refuses to grant an Accompanied Pass

____ 20. Bromden's belief that he is small is indicative of
(a) his low self-esteem
(b) a hatred of his heritage
(c) the impact of his father's hostility
(d) his declining physical health

Name _____

*One Flew Over the Cuckoo's Nest*
Final Test, Level Two
page 3

____ 21. The reactions of the service station attendants to the mental patients on their way to the fishing trip can be described in all BUT which of the following ways?
(a) accepting/obliging
(b) suspicious/manipulative
(c) angry/taunting
(d) rejecting/deceiving

____ 22. Nurse Ratched counteracts McMurphy's positive effect on the other patients by
(a) spreading rumors about his mental incompetence
(b) harassing the patients
(c) causing him to lose his temper
(d) implying that only he profits from his dealings with the patients

____ 23. All BUT which of the following occurs when McMurphy begins to talk to the others about strength and the control panel?
(a) Bromden believes McMurphy will tell the others how he helped Bromden get his strength back.
(b) McMurphy takes bets from the others that no one can lift the panel.
(c) McMurphy explains to the others how Bromden's strength has returned.
(d) Bromden thinks McMurphy will prove he doesn't do everything for money.

____ 24. Bromden realizes that he will regain his sanity
(a) after he lifts the control panel
(b) when he refuses EST
(c) when he returns from the fishing trip
(d) when he wills himself not to retreat into the fog after EST

____ 25. Nurse Ratched has McMurphy returned to the ward after EST because
(a) she wants to prove his vulnerability to the other patients
(b) she plans to order a lobotomy for him
(c) the other patients beg her to do so
(d) she plans to release him to rid the ward of his influence

____ 26. Which of the following does NOT occur during the Saturday night party?
(a) The men get drunk.
(b) Billy Bibbit sleeps with Candy.
(c) McMurphy does not participate in the revelry.
(d) Harding ingeniously prevents the supervisor from discovering their party.

Name _____

*One Flew Over the Cuckoo's Nest*
Final Test, Level Two
page 4

**C. Short Answer:** Write brief answers to the following. (2 points each)

27. Identify three of Nurse Ratched's methods of controlling the ward patients.

28. What does Nurse Ratched's first reference to Mr. Taber foreshadow?

29. Explain the analogy of the Group Meeting to a pecking party.

30. Identify three ways in which Nurse Ratched emotionally emasculates her patients.

31. Explain the symbolism of the EST table and the probes with which the shock is administered.

32. Identify two things the Combine symbolizes.

33. Describe McMurphy's undershorts and explain what you think they symbolize.

34. Explain what the fog symbolizes to Bromden.

35. Give one example of McMurphy's overt sexuality and one example of Nurse Ratched's repressed sexuality.

36. Why is McMurphy's conversation with the lifeguard significant, and how does McMurphy change because of it?

37. Identify three positive results of the fishing trip.

Name _____

**One Flew Over the Cuckoo's Nest**
Final Test, Level Two
page 5

38. Explain the cause and effect of McMurphy's attack on Washington.

39. What memories fill Bromden's mind during EST, and why are they significant?

40. Identify the event that precedes McMurphy's attack on Nurse Ratched and explain the symbolism of the attack.

41. What happens to McMurphy in the resolution of the novel? Why does this happen?

**D. Characterization:** Choose one of the following. (20 points)

1. Write a three-paragraph characterization of Randle Patrick McMurphy. Explain what he is like at the beginning of the novel, identify circumstances that lead to the development of his character, and explain what he is like at the end.

2. Write a three-paragraph paper in which you describe McMurphy's role as a martyr. Cite specific examples of symbolism from the novel.

**E. Essay:** Choose three of the following and respond to each in a well-developed paragraph of at least 5 sentences. (4 points each)

1. Explain Bromden's decline into his life as a deaf mute.
2. Explain the portrayal of sexuality in the novel. Cite specific examples.
3. Explain Kesey's portrayal of women in the novel. Cite specific examples.
4. Quote the children's rhyme from which the title of the novel is taken and explain the symbolism of the title.
5. Summarize the resolution of the novel.

**F. Creative Response:** Respond to one of the following. (12 points)

1. Write a short sequel in which Bromden and Harding have a reunion five years after the end of the novel.
2. Rewrite the story in the form of a poem or a song.
3. Write a newspaper feature article about reforms in the mental hospital following McMurphy's death. Include quotes from former patients.

# Answer Key

**Activities #1–#2:** Responses will vary.

**Study Guide**
**Part One, pp. 9–41:** 1. Chief Bromden: large half-Indian, pretends to be a deaf mute, hallucinates; Nurse Ratched: antagonist, head nurse, stern, manipulative; McMurphy: protagonist, strong, bold, aggressive; Chief Broom because he sweeps most of the time 2. retreats into a mental fog; Responses will vary. 3. Oregon mental hospital, oppressive, frightening; Responses will vary. 4. Acutes: hope for a cure; Chronics: no hope for a cure; Acutes: Harding, Bibbit, Sefelt; Chronics: Bromden, Ellis, Ruckly, Colonel Matterson; Acute 5. Combine; the ward is a factory for the Combine; Responses will vary. 6. make them subdued and compliant, then dismiss them; fear, humiliation, drugs, EST, and lobotomy 7. former patient; dismissed after lobotomy left him compliant 8. Responses will vary.

**pp. 42–69:** 1. reveals information about patients from her "spies," humiliates patients; lose himself in the fog; wants to see how McMurphy responds 2. 35 years old, never married, Korean War veteran, arrested on numerous charges; taunts her, doesn't condescend to her 3. repeated outbursts of passion suggest possible diagnosis of psychopath 4. subservient, ineffective, secretly pleased with McMurphy's brashness; Responses will vary. 5. chicken's pecking party; Responses will vary. 6. rabbits; patients accept roles as weaker elements of society who need to be controlled by a strong person. 7. subdued, afraid, won't challenge Ratched; she always wins and can make things worse; Responses will vary. 8. "get her goat," conquer Ratched with mind games; $10.00 9. Responses will vary. 10. Responses will vary.

**pp. 70–101:** 1. thinks Big Nurse can set clock at variable speeds, believes she can pipe gas and fog into ward; thinks floor moves downward, hallucinates 2. rust and ashes; Responses will vary. 3. jokes with them, gambles with them and lets them win, shakes hands with them; makes him believe the fog is gone 4. music is always loud, patients rarely allowed to hear news, protesting will get a patient branded Assaultive 5. black satin covered with white whales with red eyes; Responses will vary. 6. walks around ward with towel wrapped around as if he is naked, then drops towel 7. get music turned down, be allowed to use another room for card games, plan a carnival for the men; gets use of tub room; Responses will vary. 8. went to same high school; Dr. Spivey becomes McMurphy's ally.

**pp. 102–128:** 1. Responses will vary. 2. airfield was fogged in for protection; doesn't want to be sent for more Electro-Shock treatments 3. drag the patients out of the fog; they will be easy to get at 4. only Cheswick and Scanlon vote to watch the World Series because others are afraid of Ratched; win money from them 5. break the window; the control panel 6. when he said "Mama"; makes him afraid and causes girls to laugh at him; Responses will vary. 7. All 20 Acutes vote "yes"; McMurphy gets Bromden to vote, making a majority; Ratched refuses request, saying the voting was closed; Responses will vary. 8. men sit in front of a blank TV screen; Responses will vary. 9. Responses will vary.

**Part Two, pp. 129–151:** 1. assigns him to latrine duty; watch the blank TV each day during World Series 2. cleans staff room during meetings; everyone thinks he is deaf 3. poisons; Responses will vary. 4. not dealing with an ordinary man; he is potentially assaultive and should be placed on the Disturbed Ward; Napoleon, Genghis Khan, Attila the Hun 5. keep him on her ward; doesn't want him to become a martyr for the others; Responses will vary. 6. begins to see and think clearly, lives in reality instead of unreality 7. He is committed, and she controls his release; becomes cooperative and submissive to her; puzzled, realize they've lost their defender; Bromden hallucinates and becomes afraid

**pp. 152–173:** 1. has a seizure; refuses to take his medicine; as a warning of what can happen if they don't take their medicine 2. tall, wears high-heeled shoes, blood red fingernails, sexually suggestive; makes no move toward her 3. intimidates, criticizes, makes sexual innuendoes; Responses will vary. 4. faces; Responses will vary. 5. A patient is strapped to a table, and electric current passes through his brain, causes him to forget things, never wants another; portions of brain are cut away 6. Brain Burning; patient loses brain cells each time electricity goes through his brain 7. a bitter, icy-hearted old woman 8. must look out for himself because he doesn't want to stay in the hospital indefinitely; understand and reveal most of them can leave if they choose to do so 9. She takes away the patients' privilege to use the tub room for card games; breaks window in Nurses' Station; Responses will vary. 10. Responses will vary.

**Part Three, pp. 174–190:** 1. politely; McMurphy has his way, and Ratched bides her time; Responses will vary. 2. refuses; breaks the window again 3. writes notes for her to find in the latrine; writes outlandish tales in log book and signs them "Anon"; sleeps late; Responses will vary. 4. Dr. Spivey; supports his request for a basketball team and a fishing trip 5. take men on a fishing trip; Candy and Sandra; posts clippings about terrible boating accidents 6. Responses will vary. 7. visitors to Indian village did not look at him or act as if they heard him; people in school quit listening to him; superiors in Army ignored him 8. His father was "big" until his mother got twice his size; his father was an Indian chief who took his white wife's last name; alcoholism 9. Responses will vary. 10. McMurphy gives him a package of gum; "Thank you"; Responses will vary. 11. to make him "big" again and give him $10.00 for the fishing trip 12. Responses will vary.

**pp. 191–218:** 1. Bromden; Responses will vary. 2. afraid of germs; implies he is scared of ocean and asks him to be captain 3. only Candy arrives with a car; Dr. Spivey takes his car 4. suspicious, reluctant to help them; tells them that the men are from the criminally insane ward on a government-authorized excursion; Responses will vary. 5. don't have a signed waiver; gets Sorensen to take the boat out anyway; Responses will vary. 6. learn to laugh again, Bromden becomes part of group, all work together and display courage; Responses will vary. 7. tells policemen they do not have jurisdiction over patients and threatens the captain with investigation about number of life jackets; Responses will vary. 8. his exhausted, strained expression; Responses will vary. 9. a Saturday night date with Candy

**Part Four, pp. 219–241:** 1. begins to imply that McMurphy's dealings with the men are always for his benefit; posts statement showing each man's financial status since McMurphy's arrival; patients begin to doubt McMurphy's motives 2. doesn't deny them, brags about gaining financial independence if he stays in hospital for a year; Responses will vary. 3. that he is as crazy as a fox, points out how much money he's won from them; asks Billy to send money to Candy; doesn't explain reason for Bromden moving the control panel 4. Responses will vary. 5. six inches; takes bets from the others after he knows Bromden can move the panel 6. cautionary cleansing of any germs from fishing trip 7. He taunts and humiliates Sorensen during forced showers; Bromden; both restrained and sent to Disturbed Ward 8. kind, compassionate, understanding; Ratched is a sick, retired Army nurse who should be fired 9. by admitting he was wrong; Responses will vary. 10. Responses will vary.

**pp. 242–259:** 1. wills himself not to go into fog, recovers quickly; Responses will vary. 2. insists they don't hurt him; jaw becomes taut, face drains of color, looks thin and scared 3. thinks he will return looking weak and vulnerable; like a boxer, announces the champ is back, resumes his pranks 4. escape; set a fire 5. Candy and Sandra arrive; men laugh, joke, become drunk, and read patients' files; Billy sleeps with Candy; men try to get McMurphy to escape, but he stays 6. close friend to Ratched, treats Billy like a child, refuses to acknowledge his age, is dominant and possessive; Responses will vary. 7. pills; Responses will vary. 8. Responses will vary.

**pp. 260–272:** 1. tell his mother 2. commits suicide; McMurphy; ironic because she is everything she accuses McMurphy of being 3. He attacks her, rips her dress, and severely injures her; he is sent for a lobotomy 4. bruised, unable to speak, fearful, has lost control; leave or transfer to another ward 5. has the comatose McMurphy returned to the ward; walk by to stare at him; smothers McMurphy; Responses will vary. 6. escapes by throwing the control panel through the window, catches a ride and heads north 7. realizes events were destined to be and everything would have happened as it did even if McMurphy had escaped

**Activity #3:** Responses will vary.

**Activity #4:** 1. cupola; others relate to something original 2. conformity; others indicate deviant behavior 3. evident; others indicate something inactive 4. literary; others relate to mental aberration 5. self-denigrating; others indicate boasting 6. silence; others relate to animal feed 7. liberate; others mean to take away 8. hydrophobia; others relate to the brain or brain disorder 9. corpuscle; others relate to liquid 10. essential; others mean to manipulate 11. automatic; others indicate a design 12. expand; others mean reduce 13. mercy; others indicate opposition 14. inoffensive; others indicate reproof 15. laboratory; others refer to surgery 16. defamation; others relate to self-assurance 17. noncompliance; others indicate acceptance 18. imprudent; others indicate rationality 19. fungi; others relate to animals 20. enclose; others indicate aversion

**Activity #5:** 1. hovel 2. keelhaul 3. fraternize 4. squalor 5. cormorants 6. turret 7. indigents 8. wistful

**Activity #6:** 1. e. 2. i 3. l 4. g 5. b 6. j 7. h 8. a 9. c 10. k 11. f 12. d

**Activity #7:** Lists will vary.

**Note:** Responses to Activities #8–#15 will vary, but suggested answers are given.

**Activity #8:** McMurphy: Statements—Somebody always tells me about the rules just when they figure I'm about to do the dead opposite. What's wrong with me around here all of a sudden? You birds act like I'm a traitor to my country; Behavior—gambles with the men, tries to improve conditions on the ward, challenges Nurse Ratched's control; Fears—staying indefinitely in mental hospital, having to fulfill his role as martyr for the other men; Thoughts—realizes Nurse Ratched's cruel control, believes he should conform in order to be released, knows he's doomed to die; Looks—big, red-haired Irishman, scarred from fights; Others' actions—patients respect him, Ratched fears him.

**Activity #9:** Nurse Ratched; controls her ward through manipulation and humiliation; driven to control by previous role as Army nurse and her repressed sexuality; name symbolic of ratchet (a tool) and wretched (miserable); actions are active, reactive, and consequential; time and place significant because treatment of mentally ill in 1950s allows her to get away with abuse; she wants to be in control and is cruel; becomes fearful after McMurphy attacks her; Responses will vary.

**Activity #10:** Chief Bromden—Beginning: stays in mental fog most of the time, apathetic, hopeless. Event #1: McMurphy arrives; puzzled, doubtful. Event #2: Bromden resists retreating into the fog when McMurphy attends his first Group Meeting; slightly hopeful. Event #3: Nurse Ratched subdues the men during their first vote to watch the World Series; scared, hopeless. Event #4: Bromden raises his hand in favor of watching the World Series during the second vote; encouraged, optimistic. Event #5: Bromden goes on the fishing trip; carefree, happy. Event #6: McMurphy returns to the ward after a lobotomy. Bromden smothers him, then escapes; strong, resolute. End: Bromden regains his sanity and his right to pursue his own life.

**Activity #11:** Dale Harding: effeminate, rejected, intimidated, educated, anxious about the future. Vera Harding: sexually overt, controlling, flirtatious, undermines husband's self-esteem. George Sorensen: fearful, obsessed with cleanliness, regains some self-esteem during fishing trip. Billy Bibbit: intimidated, uncertain about his sexuality, stutters, under mother's control, hopeless. Dr. Spivey: irresolute, under Ratched's control, finds strength to support McMurphy. Candy: attractive, prostitute, friendly, accommodating. Mr. Turkle: hospital night aide, kind, understanding, not intimidated by Ratched. Geever, Washington, and Williams: hospital aides, cruel, manipulative, subservient to Ratched.

**Activity #12:** Characters: Randle Patrick McMurphy, Nurse Ratched, Chief Bromden, other patients and staff members. Setting: Oregon mental hospital, late 1950s. Conflict: Nurse Ratched maliciously controls the men on the ward through humiliation and manipulation. Events: (1) McMurphy challenges her authority. (2) McMurphy struggles with the need for self-preservation versus the need to free the men from Ratched's control. (3) McMurphy's conflict with Ratched erupts after Billy Bibbit commits suicide. Climax: McMurphy attacks and seriously injures Ratched. Resolution: Bromden smothers McMurphy after a lobotomy leaves him comatose, most of the other patients transfer to another ward or leave the hospital, and Bromden escapes.

**Activity #13:** Result: McMurphy's Death; Causes: (1) He challenges Nurse Ratched's authority and gets permission to use the tub room. (2) He gets the other patients to stage a silent protest after Ratched denies them the privilege of watching the World Series. (3) He attacks Washington when he humiliates Sorensen. (4) Ratched orders a lobotomy for him after he attacks her.

**Activity #14:** (1) McMurphy arrives: surprise, apprehension. (2) He attends his first Group Meeting: oppression, disgust, anger. (3) He displays his whale-covered shorts before Ratched; satisfaction (his); suppressed anger (hers). (4) He clashes with Nurse Ratched over watching the World Series; determination, satisfaction (his), apprehension, loathing (hers). (5) McMurphy learns that he is a "committed" patient; worried, submissive. (6) McMurphy breaks the window in the Nurses' Station; determination (his), anxiety (hers). (7) McMurphy takes the men on a fishing expedition; happiness, satisfaction, anticipation. (8) McMurphy attacks Ratched; rage (his), fear (hers).

**Activity #15:** Problem: Problems at the state mental hospital need to be corrected. Solutions: (1) Patients get a lawyer and file a formal complaint with the state hospital board. (2) Dr. Spivey arranges for McMurphy to be released so he can reveal the truth. (3) Bromden goes before the state board and reveals what he's heard in the staff meetings. (4) McMurphy gets a lawyer and files a complaint against Nurse Ratched. (5) McMurphy leads the patients in an open rebellion. Criteria: (a) Will it benefit anyone? (b) Will it cause changes in the mental hospital? (c) Will it hurt anyone? (d) Is it legal? (e) Is it feasible?

**Activity #16:** Responses will vary.

**Quiz #1:** 1. e 2. d 3. f 4. b 5. c 6. a 7. F 8. T 9. F 10. T 11. T 12. F 13. F 14. T 15. T

**Quiz #2:** 1. He is a sex maniac. 2. Combine 3. singing 4. white whales 5. turn the music down 6. Dr. Spivey 7. They are afraid Ratched will make things harder for them. 8. throwing the control panel through the window 9. Mama 10. sitting in front of the blank TV

**Quiz #3:** 1. T 2. F 3. T 4. F 5. F 6. T 7. poison 8. Others will think he is a martyr. 9. He no longer feels fogged in and can see things clearly. 10. He finds out he is committed, and she is the one who can release him. 11. Electro-Shock Therapy and lobotomy 12. takes away patient's privilege for using tub room; breaks window in Nurses' Station

**Quiz #4:** 1. basketball 2. he gives him a package of chewing gum 3. his mother made him so small he couldn't fight anymore 4. move the control panel 5. Candy, Dr. Spivey 6. Nurse Ratched denies his request for an Accompanied Pass. 7. puts up clippings about horrible boating accidents on the ocean 8. Others started acting like he was too dumb to hear, see, or say anything. 9. tells him they need him to be captain of the boat and implies he's afraid of the ocean 10. took the boat without permission; Dr. Spivey threatens an investigation into shortage of life jackets

**Quiz #5:** 1. T 2. T 3. F 4. F 5. T 6. T 7. T 8. F 9. F 10. T 11. Bromden smothers him when he returns to the ward comatose after a lobotomy. 12. severely injured; returns to ward but has lost control 13. escapes by throwing control panel through window 14. checks himself out 15. transfers to another ward

**Final Test, Level One:** **A.** 1. d 2. i 3. a 4. e 5. b 6. j 7. f 8. c 9. g 10. h **B.** 11. c 12. b 13. a 14. c 15. d 16. b 17. d 18. a 19. c 20. d 21. b 22. a 23. c 24. b 25. d 26. b 27. c 28. a 29. d 30. b 31. b 32. a 33. d 34. b 35. a 36. c 37. b 38. d 39. c 40. a 41. b 42. d 43. a 44. c 45. d **C. & D.:** Responses will vary.

**Final Test, Level Two:** **A.** 1. loud, strong, brash, protagonist 2. half-Indian, hallucinates, low self-esteem, narrator 3. intimidating, cruel, manipulative, antagonist 4. insecure, educated, dominated by wife 5. weak, insecure, intimidated, subservient to mother 6. ineffective, subservient, intimidated 7. suggestive, flirtatious, degrades husband 8. afraid of germs, humiliated 9. black aides, filled with hate, cruel 10. feels ashamed and guilty, repressed **B.** 11. c 12. d 13. a 14. c 15. b 16. a 17. d 18. c 19. b 20. a 21. a 22. d 23. c 24. d 25. a 26. c **C.** 27. intimidation, fear, covert actions, humiliation 28. McMurphy's lobotomy 29. Ratched exposes Harding's weakness (the "blood") and others begin to peck him to pieces as chickens peck a weak, blood-covered chicken to death. 30. reveals their secret weaknesses, gets patients to confess to sexual aberrations, gets them to spy and report on each other 31. Patients are strapped to a table shaped like a cross and receive a crown of electric sparks, symbolic of Christ's crucifixion. 32. government, forces of society, mental hospital 33. black satin covered with white whales with red eyes; whales symbolize untamed power or force of good as in *Moby Dick* 34. his mental retreat from humiliation or anything that hurts him 35. McMurphy: sexual innuendoes, deck of cards; Ratched: concealed breasts 36. McMurphy discovers he is committed and can only be released by Ratched; becomes submissive to her 37. men laugh again, Sorensen gains self-confidence, Bromden becomes part of group, all work together 38. Cause: Washington humiliates Sorensen by trying to force him to accept cleansing treatment. Effect: Washington is injured, Bromden joins McMurphy; both are sent to Disturbed Ward for EST 39. Air Raid; hunting birds with his father during childhood, conflict between his mother and father over Indian traditions, childhood rhyme "One flew over the cuckoo's nest..."; reveal details about his childhood; foreshadow his escape 40. Billy Bibbit commits suicide; attack exposes her breasts and symbolizes figurative exposure of her repressed sexuality and intimidation of men 41. Bromden smothers him because a lobotomy has left him comatose. **D.–F.:** Responses will vary.